The Sliding Door

By Dora Wright

Foreword

Thank you for buying my book. It is so exciting to see it in print. I live near beautiful Loch Lomond in the West of Scotland.
I've been writing poetry since 2009 and have been published in newspapers, magazines and online events and I enjoy reading at Open Mic nights.
I am a member of three writers groups which keep me busy.
My interests are walking, the cinema and live theatre. My passion is reading Crime books.
This book about life, love and laughter is my first and hopefully not my last. I hope you enjoy reading it as much as I did writing it.

Acknowledgements

I would like to thank my good friend Christine Robertson for her inspiration, dedication and patience in editing and help publishing this book.

Contents

09. The Sliding Door

10. After the Love has Gone

11. When the Bluebells ur Oot

13. Moonglow

15. Sometimes

16. No one Will Mourn Me

17. Daily Bread

18. She

19. Down in the Woods

21. All the Colours of Darkness

22. Twilight Zone

23. The Scent of Night

24. Wally Dug

25. Love

26. Wullie's Bucket

28. Moonbeam Shimmer

29. The Linesman

30. The Midnight Hour

31. Granny and the Wolf

33. Baked to Perfection

34. Where Mermaids Sleep

35. My Friend the Tree

36. Foraging

38. Just Dreaming

39. Flatulence

40. The Ghost Fields

41. The Shower

42. On the road to Damascus

43. Chair of Dreams

44. Tell the Rain to Stop!!

45. The Gathering Darkness

46. Ginger Thief

47. Alone in the Garden

48. Wee Moira

49. The Booler

51. A Taste of Summer

52. Siren's Song

53. Being a Traffic Warden

54. The Pool

56. Leaving

57. Unicorn

59. A Dead Good Job

61. Regrets

62. Ther's Somethin' up Mah nose

63. Dustbin Man

65. The Kissing Trees

66. A Lifetime of Dying Slowly

67. Love Crossed

68. A Song for the Dying

69. Just a Bad Dream

71. Peaceful garden

72. Butterfly Morning

73. Mixed up Murder

75. Only One Shoe

76. Tea the Panacea

77. The Bees Farewell

78. Autonomy

79. Had Enough

80. The Perfume of Angels

81. Fishing for Compliments

82. Beg Me

83. Tattoo

The Sliding Door

The sliding door from here to there
is beckoning me to step on through
I don't know if I'm ready
I don't know what to do
What if there's nothing there,
What if it's all a lie
What if there's nothing after
What if you just fade away and die
We've been led to believe there's a paradise
Where all our dreams come true
Where all our family is waiting
Waiting for us to come through
But what if it's all a lie
What if there's nothing after
What if I step through and all I hear is the sound of the Devils laughter

After the Love has Gone

After the love has gone
I lie spread out
under the wind
talking to the dead

This thing of darkness
assails my senses,
the scents of night
cocoon me

My tears flow freely
seeping into the earth
You're dead
lie beneath me

I'm alone with the wind

When the Bluebells ur Oot

When the bluebells ur oot
An' spread oot a' aboot
An' the hills ur a' blue
An' the hedgerows ur fu'
It's heaven withoot a doot

In the spring when burds a' sing
An' trees turn green
Ther a sight tae be seen
What joy they bring
Summer's sultry days

When butterflies play
The bees buzz aroon'
fae bloom tae bloom
an' midgies
come oot tae play

Autumn colours hard tae beat
Leaves a' alang the street
Crackle in the mornin' breeze
Fallin' doon fae the trees
Noo they're obsolete

Frosty mornin's decorate
Branches an' the garden gate
Robin starts tae sing again
Mappin' oot his wee domain
Till nature reincarnate

Moonglow

It was the band playing" Moonglow"
that was messing with my head
instead of dancing here with her
I should be in my bed

Her perfume wafts around me
and her lips are ruby red
her dress is tight and sexy
I feel a kind of dread

The music's slow and bluesy
her body's pressed to mine
she's moving slow and sultry
I need a glass of wine

I feel my passion rising
I just can't take much more
So before I change my mind
I whisk her out the door

The alley's dark and quiet
I give her one last chance
she runs her fingers down me
in a merry little dance

I get her up against the wall
and fuck her till she yells
she whispers up against my mouth
"Is that the 'Round Two' bell?"

I think I've made a bloomer
I just can't stand the pace
I've got to get away from her,
but she notices my face

She wiggles to the doorway
and turns to blow a kiss
then bends her little finger
I say "don't you take the piss."

I'm going home I've had enough
I stagger down the alley
I know I'm only forty two
but that felt like a finale

Sometimes

Sometimes
I'd love to scream and shout
and throw things

Sometimes
I can understand
How people get frustrated
Lose the head – lash out

Sometimes
It's hard to hold it all together
Ignore the hurtful words
The awful silences

Sometimes
A raised voice isn't always the loudest

No One will Mourn Me

No one will mourn me
No one will care
No one will notice
that I'm not there

I'm invisible
Don't rate a call
Don't rate a visit
from anyone at all

They'll just give a sigh
and say "That's too bad."
But no one will care
Isn't that sad?

She

She glows like the stars
On a cold dark night
Radiant of face,
Eyes so bright
Beckoning me onwards
Towards the mound where she sits
Regal and proud
Surrounded by angels
Singing

She opens her arms
Drawing me near
to the warmth
She keeps within.
Wiping the tears that fall from my face
With fingers so light, and a smile full of love
that fills my heart
with hope

I sit at her feet
Head bowed
Angelic goodness
surrounding me like an aura
Stars fall from the heavens, as the vision
fades away
and I cry with happiness
at the blessing I've been given

Daily Bread

Her floury hands
The smell of yeast
Has me rising
to the occasion
She kneads me
Shaping me
Breathes life into me,
I explode into shape
She smiles at her handiwork
Samples the fruits of her labour

Down in the Woods

If you go down in the woods today
You're sure of a big surprise
There's things going on in the woods today
You'll never believe your eyes,
There's people parking in their cars
Some who've stumbled out from bars
Come to see the action there
Come to see some bodies bare
There's "dogging" happening everywhere
Down in the woods today.

If you go down to the woods today
It's best to go in your car
And take along binoculars
You won't have to travel far

The word goes round they all arrive
Who said you shouldn't drink and drive?
They park their cars in open view
So you can share the action too
You should see the things they do
Down in the woods today

If you go down to the woods today
You'll get an education
From one on one, to three at play
And there's some oral stimulation

There 's even cans of dairy whipped cream
That splatter the windows covered with steam
As "Dogger's" move from car to car
Watching action completely bizarre
Underneath the old "Dog Star"
Down in the woods today

All the Colours of Darkness

All the colours of darkness
swirl around my head,
weaving in and out of dreams
as I lie here on my bed.

I thought dying would be painful
but it doesn't seem to be,
its like floating through the universe
and feeling really free.

My past and all my memories
appear before my eyes,
places, people, laughter, tears,
go quickly passing by.

Colours of the rainbow
brighten up my room,
chasing away the darkness,
chasing away the gloom.

The sunlight's warm and tender,
my thoughts are light and gay
a last breath passes by my lips
and slowly drifts away

Twilight Zone

I knew it had to happen
I thought I was prepared
to follow the path ahead
but I was really scared

They started me on pills
to help prepare the way
they made me feel so ill
all I did was sit and pray

But pills were just the start
the journey took me years
along the way I had to learn
to throw away my fears

Now I am complete
a woman I've become
no longer in the mirror
will I see my mother's son.

The Scent of Night

The Scent of night cocoons us
Your skin tastes of honey
As I run the tip of my tongue up your spine
enticing you to notice me again
Sweat runs from your body to mine
I ache for you with every breath I take
Wanting to feel your weight on my body
again
Your arms around me
Your lips fastened to mine
The scent of night is hypnotic
Weaving spells of enchantment
Passion is carried on the breeze
and you and I
must enjoy every heavenly moment

Wally Dug

The Wally dug stood on the shelf,
all alone by itself.
People said, "There should be two."
"Yes, said I, but one will do."
But "Wally dugs come in pairs
the other one of him's not there."
"I know, said I, it went astray,
on the day my man went away."
"Maybe he took it just for spite."
"Yes, I said I, you could be right."

The other dug is buried deep,
in the grave where my man sleeps.
I stopped my man from bashing me,
buried him beneath the tree,
by his side the Wally dug lies,
It hit my man between the eyes,
saved me from a life of pain,
my man will not bash me again.
My Wally Dug upon the shelf,
like me is happy by itself.

Love

Love, oh love
What it does to us
Gives us cravings
for things we can't have
and moments we want
to last forever
It lifts our spirits
in anticipation
Leaves us crying
in desperation
Love, oh love
is a giver of pain
Cutting our heart
into little pieces
with thoughtless words
we didn't want to hear
Making our dreams disappear
Leaving us in tears

Wullie's Bucket

Wullie had an auld tin bucket
He kept it by the back door
His Mither filled it wae bleach and watter
when she slunged the kitchen floor

He turned it upside doon tae sit on
and he used it tae collect the eggs
He stood on it to clean the windaes
as he hud such wee short legs

His mither carried coal in it
to make the coal fire reek
and it came in really handy when the
the roof had sprung a leak

His bucket was a useful tool
It was great when picking berries
His mither made terrific wine
and Wullie would get quite merry

One day he found a little moose
That had fell inside his bucket
At first he was going to kill it
an' then he thought, aw "fuck it"

He tipped it oot and it ran away
towards the garden shed
If his mither knew whit he had done
her face wid turn bright red

He rubbed his haun's the gither
thought that's a good deed done
then sat upon his bucket,
tae enjoy the morning sun

Moonbeam Shimmer

Among the moonbeams I watched her sway
shimmering and dancing the night away
Her body twisting this way and that
supple and lively as a Siamese cat

All around the trees she danced
like a marionette entranced
Ethereal in the pale moons glow
a translucent and ephemeral show
Flowing with the winds vibrations
reveling in the new sensations
Remembering when she lived her dream
of dancing on the silver screen
Night's of passion and adoration
filled her mind at each gyration
How long she thought,
will this feeling last
how long until I finally pass
My body free at last to roam
and dance towards my heavenly home

I watched her floating to the sky
rejoicing in her last goodbye
Becoming one with stars and moon
Softly humming her favourite tune

The Linesman

I watch the linesman line the pitch
and wonder if he ever gets the itch
To paint instead patterns exotic
or would that be just too chaotic?
Surely he must want to rebel
wish straight lines would go to hell
He could create an intricate maze
maybe start a brand new craze
I bet his thoughts must go soaring
thinking white's a trifle boring
Time for him to make a change
even if folk think it strange
Give the players a brand new view
by using colours of every hue
Make a spiral round and round
filling up the football ground
or give the club a bit of class
with a Banksy on the grass

But no, he'd better toe the line
get footballer's on the pitch in time
So lines of white on patch of green
is all that's ever to be seen

The Midnight Hour

At the midnight hour when the clock stops chiming
and the night is dark and your heart is pining
To hear his voice, but he isn't there
and you sit in fear upon your chair
In the distance you hear a dog bark
making you think of that night in the park
When the moon was high and he was by your side
When you were young and full of pride
He took your hand and kissed your lips
so feather light like an angels sips
He took your love and left you lying
cold and alone as your heart was dying
He thought that he could walk away
never dreamt he'd have to pay
for ripping your sheltered life apart
As you stuck a knife in his black, black heart
You buried him in a shallow grave
A fitting place for a heartless knave
Now every night when darkness falls
and shadows move against your wall
Peace of mind is what you crave
as you think of him in that cold dark grave

Granny and the Wolf

Why don't you come to see me?
My granny said to me
She's a dab hand at the texting
Said she had a right sore knee
I said I'd come tomorrow
And she said she'd bake a cake
one for us to have with tea
and topped with almond flakes
I loaded up my basket
with some treats to take along
and a CD of Jimmy Nail
she really likes his songs
I took the shortcut through the woods
And got to granny's house
I should visit her more often
I felt a total louse

She was really pleased to see me
But her mouth it looked enormous
Then I spotted what was wrong
It was her teeth, they were ginormous
She sat me down and told me
She'd got some new false teeth
She couldn't quite get used to them
Things got stuck underneath
I told her to take them out
And put her old ones in
She did and looked much happier
Threw the new ones in the bin

I asked if she'd seen the wolf
she said she'd shot it dead
For killing all her chickens
when it broke into her shed
Nothing granny does surprises me
She's a law unto herself
I said I'd text when I got home
She said... please yourself.

Baked to Perfection

His hands leave a trace of flour,
on my face, my neck, my shoulders
Later I shall look at them
Remember how skilful he was
A master of his craft

On the floor
next to my clothes
His baker's whites lie discarded
Our passions rise without the need for yeast
Proving by the moment

Where Mermaids Sleep

Way down deep is a cavern full of light
where mermaids come together
to sing in sweet delight
A siren song so beautiful
and soothing to the ear
haunting notes that fill the air
to draw us ever near

I thought that I could visit them
and swam below the waves
Hoping I could join with them
in that bright and secret cave
The sunlight was sparkling
down there in the deep
in that cavern full of light
where all the mermaids sleep

They made me welcome, smiled at me
as they sang their mournful song
In the cavern I could breath
and I began to sing along
But soon the light began to fade
and the tide began to turn
I was trapped beneath the waves
never to return.

My Friend the Tree

I sit beneath the falling leaves
mourning summer's passing
all around the maple tree
its leaves are all amassing
Its cosy sitting here
sheltering from the rain
I lean my back against the tree
I'm sure he feels my pain

He's stood here many years
and I've sat here many times
He always brings me comfort
this patriarch in his prime
Sometimes I think he answers me
when I tell him of my woes
I pretend for every tear I've cried
another leaf does grow

Perhaps the leaves all around
are children of my tears
I like to think we've had a bond
through all these many years
I hug the tree before I go
because he is my friend
Inside I feel him hug me back
and then I homeward wend

Foraging

My man he liked to forage
in the hedgerows and the woods
He said the things he found
were the very best of foods

He brought me home ripe berries
of every kind of hue
Wild garlic and fresh mushrooms
and a truffle or two

He collected wild elder flowers
and made some lovely wine
He picked up windfall apples
most of them looked fine

I baked them in a pie for him
to have with cold ice cream
he always praised my pastry
said I cooked just like a dream

Then he started up a group
they had a lot of fun
They found lots of things to gather
along the rushing burn

And then he gathered along the way
a woman he couldn't resist
Started sneaking off with her
to have a wee sly kiss

I wasn't putting up with that
I dropped a hint or two
but he was too loved up to notice
there was nothing I could do

I served him up his favourite meal
of steak and wild mushroom pie
If he'd stuck to gathering berries
he wouldn't have had to die

                                    faraway
                                    ns grey
                                    e Milky Way

                         ... shiny and bright
of rainbows and unicorns ghostly white
Hanging together in the starry night
like something from Brigadoon

I dreamed of drifting along on a cloud
reciting my poetry right out loud
Of angels and cherubs looking on proud
and whistling away like a loon

I dreamed as I lay on my bed alone
of those who live in a different zone
Of others like me whose thought's had flown
Wrapped up in a silken cocoon

I dreamed till my dream drifted away
left to me wonder in the cold light of day
Why nothing on earth looked half as gay
but more like a wet afternoon

Flatulence

The flatulence
caused by over indulgence
made my stomach bloat
As I let rip another one
the duvet started to float
It floated over to the door
and then there came a shout
what the hell is that bloody smell
open a window...let it out
I had a little giggle
didn't say a word
he said "Did you do that?"
I said "Don't be absurd."
He said "Do you think we've got a gas leak
should I phone an engineer?"
I said "You're being paranoid.
have you been on the beer?"
Come to bed and get some sleep
I'm putting out the light
then I let rip another one
it gave him such a fright
I couldn't stop from laughing
his face it was a sight
He said "There's not a chance in hell
I'm sleeping with you tonight"
I'm going to the spare room,
I'll see you in the morning
if you're still as toxic tomorrow

shout and give me a warning
The Ghost Fields

The ghost fields lie waiting
for you to walk by,
to lure you inside
with an inhuman cry
Not everyone hears it
only those near the end,
those pitiful creatures
with hurts that won't mend.

The ghost fields are full
of souls terrifying
that listened too long
to the cries of the dying

For ghosts of the dead
don't all lie at rest
They patrol the ghost fields
as the sun sets in the west

So if you hear cries
from the fields all around,
just scurry on by
with your eyes to the ground,
Don't listen to them
as they grumble and cry,
shout out as you go,
"Not my time to die."

The Shower

I watch him as he showers
shampooing his hair
sponging his body slowly
from top to bottom
I ask if he needs help
he smiles knowingly
shaking his head
Rivulets of water
run down him as
he stands there
washing the shampoo
from his hair
I hold out a towel
he wraps it around his waist
then takes me in his arms
and kisses me
takes my hand
leads me to the bedroom
where the candles burn
 in anticipation

On the Road to Damascus

On the road to my Damascus
I met a man with velvet eyes
who touched me on the forehead
forgave me all my lies

He talked about his travels
to countries far and wide
of people of every race
and how he was their guide

My heart he filled with love
then told me of his vow
to rid the world of hatred
but he had to leave me now

He said I shouldn't be afraid
to walk the road alone
he would be right by my side
and handed me a stone

He said to always carry it
that no one was without sin
so be careful not to judge
lest you know what lies within

He left me with a brother's kiss
said we'd meet again some day
that he'd always travel with me

if I needed him, just pray
Chair of Dreams

I open the door, I see the chair
sometimes I wish it wasn't there
It was enchanted or so it seemed
it wove such love into my dreams
wrapped me in a warm cocoon
as I gazed out at the silver moon

I'd prayed to be a family
build for us a family tree
but when he saw what I'd created
it lit a fuse, I was berated
this chair is just a chair he said
all these things are in your head

You've made this room something it's not
filled it with toys, a chair, a cot
This is your dream, it's not mine
I don't want to share you, or your time
just you and I, a couple, a pair
no one else to share our lair

Now the room is empty and bare
we're all alone, me and my chair

Tell the Rain to Stop!!

It's been pourin doon aw thru the night
pouring doon wae a' it's might
somethin' disnae seem quite right
please tell the rain tae stop

A' aroon's an' air o' chill
The watters runnin' doon the hill
the coo's ur staunin' awfy still
Please tell the rain tae stop

A' the drains ur overflowin'
in the gerden nothins' growin'
the wind is cauld an'wildly blowin
please, tell the rain tae stop

Ah cannae open up mah door
av never seen rain like this afore
ma body's shaken tae the core
Please tell the rain tae STOP!

The rain is really pourin' doon
ma heid is goin roon an' roon
ah feel its gonnae burst right soon
please tell the rain tae stop

God! Ahm on ma knees tae pray
ahm scared ma hoose wull float away
ah cannae staun this wan mer day

Tell the fuckin' rain tae stop...
The Gathering Darkness

The gathering darkness hides my face
I wish it could hide my soul
let me forget the things I've seen
let me play another roll
let me be my other self
let me shine with love and grace
let others see the inner me
let them see my other face

This face I wear to fool myself
hides memories from long ago
but still they linger deep inside
they will not let me go
I wear a smile to fool myself
I hope I fool you too
it's the only way I can survive
the things that were taboo

One day the hurts will go away
light from my face will shine
I feel that day is coming soon
and happiness will be mine
I'll have no need for darkness
my head I'll hold up high
my soul will weep with happiness
and stars will fill the sky

Ginger Thief

Ah saw a boy who had rid herr
ah turned aroon he wisnae ther
ah turned wance mer an' ther he wis
riding a bike that wisnae his
It wisnae his that ah knew
as soon as he came in tae view
cause it was mine the cheeky toad
two fingers up tae me he showed

Ah shouted hey git aff mah bike
use yer legs an' take a hike
but he kept peddlin' doon the street
ah tried tae run but ah wis beat
But then good fortune came tae call
he wisnae lookin' an hit a wa'
he went flyin' battered his heid
wis lucky he didnae end up died

Ah picked him up gied him a shake
telt him he wis a slimy wee snake
then let him go cause he wis greetin'
ah shoulda gied him a bliddy beatin'
Ah grabbed ma bike an' walked on hame
mah bike wid never be the same
because a boy who hud rid herr
hudnae money fur his ferr

Alone in the Garden

Alone I sit in the summer sun
and give a heartfelt sigh
watching flitting butterflies
and bees buzz quietly by
What bliss it is to have a place
where one can sit at ease
with beauty all around
and feel a cooling breeze
Chirping birds sing with glee
as others soar above
While on the fence -
with amorous intent
sits a pair of cooing doves
An iridescent dragonfly
swoops by the goldfish pond
seeking flies and midges
for him to feast upon
soon the sun will disappear
and I'll hear the blackbirds song
bidding farewell to the day, in this haven
where I belong

Wee Moira

We Moira wis the best o' a'
at singin' oot that song sae braw
People came frae miles aroon
tae hear her beltin' oot that tune
She sang it maist on New Year's Eve
oh whit a bonnie web she'd weave
She brought a tear tae every eye
frae Elgin tae the Isle o' Skye
She sang o' mist abune the brae
an' a' aboot a wee hoose tae
She sang o' loved ones far away
remembered fondly every day
Aye Moira brought them a' the gither
wae a song o' hame an' heather
for jist a while on New Year's Eve
a' ther grief behind they'd leave
They sat so still and no one spoke
till Moira finished "My Ain Folk"

(Wee Moira refers to Moira Anderson of
The White Heather Club)

The Booler

My man he is a booler
boolin' is his game
he'd rather be at the the boolin' club
instead o' being hame

He's got trophies aw aroon the hoose
that he polishes tae a shine
but dare ah suggest he dis the brasses
naw, that's wher he draws the line

His meals ur taken at a run
when ther's tournaments tae play
hisnae got any time tae waste
he's got games tae win the day

If he disnae win a cup or two
he'll kick up sich a din
boot the cat, slam the door
tae let me know he's in

He's so bloody predictable
if he wins he'll celebrate
ah'll no see him till the bar's shut
an he staggers in the gate

Ahm fed up sittin at hame masel
watchin' rubbish on TV
A wish he'd get anither hobby
an' spend mer time wae me

Oor sex life is a shambles
he cannae get an erection
maybe ah should take up boolin'
join the wumman's section

A Taste of Summer

You can taste summer
It assaults the senses making
subliminal links and
complex associations that
fire up your brain

The aromas of summer
are heady and sensual
Fruits and berries flavour
your mouth with wild sweetness
evoking forgotten memories

One deep breath and you're
smelling the honeyed sweetness
of the buddleia
and walking in gardens of
night scented Stock

Nights are full of erotic sensations
bodies bare and glistening
rivulets of sweat waiting
to tease tongues
tasting of salt and love

Siren's Song

Beneath the sea
where sirens sing
a song to chill the soul
The tattooist of Auschwitz sits
tattooing a lemon sole
He'd like to paint the fish one day
in bizarre splashes of colour
but black squid ink is all he has
could death be any crueller
He recalls the fences
the smoke, the smell
the bodies gaunt
a living hell
He remembers his paper aeroplane
soaring through the air
Watching his childhood dreams
with feelings of despair
All love was gone
hope gone too
no reason to go on
The lemon sole drifted away
once more
he was
alone

Being a Traffic Warden

Ah really love mah job,
but ah get a lotta stick
from a' they moanin' drivers
that tell me ahm a prick
Ah tell them ther's signs oan the street
tae say ther's nae parking ther
but they think signs don't apply tae them
an' they jist park withoot a care

They come oot wae a' the excuses
but av heard them a' afore
dae they think ma heid zips up the back?
Then they try a wee bit o' rapport
"Ah wis only nippin' tae the shop
fur a can o' Irn Bru
an' tae get the mornin' paper
ah only took a minute or two."

They rant an' rave as ah write the ticket
an' stick it oan ther car
Ah can hear them shoutin' efter me
afore ah get too far
These guys should a' be on the stage
It's like a bliddy farce
when ther fine comes thru ther door
they can stick it up ther arse!

The Pool

On summer nights when the moon is full
and something stirs in a deep dark pool
you feel the air begin to stir
and you pause a moment to think of her
when she walked amongst the forest trees
her perfume wafting on the breeze
the way she'd smile and whisper your name
while playing one of her crazy games
telling you tales of her mystic powers
as she lay with you among the flowers
making you feel you could touch the stars
ride on a unicorn, fly to Mars

She'd weave such fantasies of delight
to entertain you through the night
then disappear as the sun arose
leaving you feeling a door had closed
shutting you out from the glories within
with a farewell kiss upon your chin
wondering when she'd re-appear
to whisper her magic in your ear
Until the day the truth was told
and the love inside your heart turned cold
then drowning her in a deep dark pool
for taking your love for the love of a fool

Now on nights when the moon is full
as stars shine down and the air is cool

you think of her and her bewitching ways
and the way she filled your lonely days
It hurts so much when true love dies
she never should have told you lies

Leaving

I said I'd leave when the wind blew south
to help me on my way
I said I'd leave when the days grew dark
with clouds of black and grey
I said I'd leave when I was bored
when life had lost its glow
I said I'd leave if you stopped smiling
if tears began to show
I said I'd leave when you said go
but I didn't see the signs
that said your love for me was gone
for me you wouldn't pine
I waited till you shut the door
placed my suitcase at my feet
I waited in the silence
and then began to weep
I waited at the station
for a train to take me south
I waited for you to come
with my hand held to my mouth
I waited for the tears to stop
for the skies to turn to blue
I waited but you never came
my heart was broken in two
I waited till the train had gone
I didn't know what to do
so I waited and I waited
and I waited

Unicorn

Unicorn, oh Unicorn why are you so sad?
Are you being punished, have you been very bad?
Your eyes are dull and empty, your coat is has lost its sheen
your mane is full of tangles, and your tail's not very clean
I want to ride upon your back up to the Astral Plane
and hobnob with the Angels before the moon doth wane
Maybe we could take a ride along the Milky Way
Oh tell me little Unicorn, what have you to say?

Pretend this is not a carousel that's turning round and round
look up to the sky above let go this earthly mound
you were made for finer things, you're not just made of wood
look at the broader picture, you can do some good
carry me to those places I've only dreamed about
you can do it if you want of that I have no doubt

Take me where the shooting stars and deep black holes are found
Free yourself from the chains that bind you to this merry go round

Don't shake your head, please don't cry, don't shed another tear
You know the only thing that's holding you back is fear
I'll polish your horn and comb your mane to make you look so nice
We could be above the rainbow in only half a trice
Free your hoofs from this man-made hell and off we'll go tonight
Your coat is gleaming once again and your eyes are sparkling bright
Let us away don't look behind, let's fly into the unknown
Well at least till nine o'clock when Mum says I must go home

A Dead Good Job

If you've got a wee deid body
and yer kinda in a jam
dinnae look nae further
buddy ahm yer man
I'll toddle 'roon an' pick it up
in ma wee black van
if yev got the readies
jist call me, Dan the Man

Ye don't huv tae know the details
o' where its goin' tae go
jist you wave bye bye tae it
jist go wae the flow
Ye'll never huv tae worry
aboot it turning up
wance its gone its gone fur good
like coffee oot a cup

This jobs a right wee goldmine
I'm a grave digger tae mah trade
every time ah dae a funeral
an extra body's laid
naebody ever notices
how deep ah dig the hole
ah'm glad they offered me this job
when ah wis on the dole

So remember if yer ever stuck
wae a body ye don't want
if yer ever in a jam
yer wishes ah kin grant
so lift yer phone gie me a call
me an' mah wee black van
ahl sort oot aw yer troubles
jist call me, Dan the Man

Regrets

Last night when in my bed I lay
looking at the moon
I remembered how your body felt
we parted far too soon

I thought you the one I'd waited for
to fill my dark cold nights
when we met it seemed like fate
our attraction felt so right

But I was wrong love didn't last
it burned out like a candle
you just couldn't stand the pace
I was too much for you to handle

But now you're gone and I'm all alone
I wish you were still here
I shouldn't have told you, you were crap
and to get your arse in gear

I was hasty please come back
I'll give you another chance
lets practice just a little more
that horizontal dance

Ther's Somethin' up Mah Nose

The blue eyed boy wae ginger herr
wis picking his nose withoot a care
he said "Ther's somethin' big stuck up ther
ah cannae thole it any mer

Wae needle nosed pliers he poked aboot
trying hard tae get it oot
but it widnae move it hud pit doon root
wis attached tae his brain withoot a doot

He tugged at it till it finally broke loose
an' ther it wis, a teeny wee moose
he recognised it, they hud called it Bruce
at night it ran aboot the hoose

Until wan day it vanished fae view
where it went naebody knew
an' aw this time he'd no' hud a clue
it wiz up his nose huvin' a chew

Still Bruce wis family he set him free
said don't come back an' bother me
if ye dae ye'll surely dee
mah nose is no' fur the likes o' thee

Dustbin Man

Ahm jist a wee dustbin man
ah walk behind the truck
emptyin' a' the dustbins
getting rid o' a' the muck

I've often thought ah'd kill the wife
an' stick her in a bin
but she's that big and fat noo
ah widnae get her in

Aw she dis is watch the tele
an' stuff herself wae junk
it costs a bomb tae keep her fed
thank god she's no' a drunk

Ah meet a lot o' folk
when ahm oan the job
maist o' them are really nice
though wan or two are snobs

Wan day ah missed a wummans bin
she gave me a tellin' aff
then she reported me -
tae ma boss - the wee nyaff

He's a right wee bliddy moaner
and he likes tae take the piss
when he's aff oan holiday
its utter bloody bliss

Still it's no a bad a wee job
keeps me oot the Bookies
a sometimes wish ah could work a' night
noo the wife's too fat fur nookie

The Kissing Trees

I'll meet you at the kissing trees
when the moon is full
we too will kiss and take a walk
down by the Mermaid Pool
perhaps we'll hear her siren song
whispered on the breeze
calling to her lover
across the raging seas

The kissing trees are where we met
when caught out by the rain
we sheltered there the two of us
and then met there again
It became our favourite place
to sit and dream together
cocooned beneath the branches
sheltered from the weather

We fell in love so easily
soul mates from the start,
you told me that you loved me
and I gave to you my heart
we've been together many years
but still you like to tease
remind me of the day we met
beneath the kissing trees

A Lifetime of Dying Slowly

My earliest memories
are of being alone
being on the outside

When others
spread their wings to fly
my wings stayed unfurled

Others met soul-mates
and fell in love
I searched for mine in vain

Year after year
I watched as my dreams
fell unnoticed by the wayside

Now that my time is running out
I am finally at peace
with myself

I don't fear death
I welcome it
I've had a lifetime of dying slowly

Love Crossed

I fancied a boy
wae ginger herr
every time I saw him
ah jist stood and stared

He wis handsome an' tall
a heid above the rest
an' Oh that ginger herr
wis whit ah loved the best

He shone like a beacon
ye cud spot him fur miles
I'd gie him the eye
try mah wummanly wiles

But' jist when ah thot
he wis the guy fur me
ah wis shattered tae hear
he'd voted SNP.

A Song for the Dying

In that room of white it was hard to see
you lying there so still
through the window the sun was shining
but around you there was an air of chill

I prayed so hard for you not to go
but you were failing and very weak
I held your hand so cold and frail
pressed it to my cheek

Never more will I hear your voice
or see your eyes so blue
never again will your lips kiss mine
and whisper I love you

I softly sing the song we loved
wipe a teardrop from my eye
kiss your cold lips once last time
and say a last goodbye

Just a Bad Dream

At the corner store he bought groceries and wine
told himself he was doing fine.
He walked each day in the local park
the children made fun of him, thought it a lark,
that he was as regular as the morning train
that took them to school and back again.

He ate his meals at set times of the day
never deviating it just was his way.
He went to bed when the clock struck ten
hot drink to hand with book and pen.
He kept a diary had done for years
wrote down the things that made him shed tears.

In the morning he'd rise refreshed
breakfast on the foods he liked best
then put on the coat he'd worn since the war
pinned on the medals he kept in the drawer
then marched down the road to the beat of a drum
limping a bit with the leg that was numb.

He'd tell himself he was on a mission
to batter the enemy into submission.
When he reached the corner shop
his leg was sore and he had to stop,
as all the memories he tried to forget
came rushing back with all the regret

He'd been lucky avoided most of the flack,
unlike those that never came back.
That's why he wore same old coat
with medals he got for sinking a boat,
he had to live this life of routine,
he couldn't remember the man he had been,
his brain was a jumble, habit ruled supreme,
the war he pretended, had been a bad dream.

Peaceful Garden

I watch him as he cuts the grass
walking up and down
a look of desperation on his face
on his forehead a frown
What is it he's thinking about
what's making him so morose
has someone dared invade his patch
stolen a favourite rose?
His garden's all he thinks about
morning noon and night
it truly is a work of art
beautiful to the sight
Every minute of every day
you'll see him bustling around
as busy as the buzzing bees
that in his flowers abound
he never has a minute to spare
he's always on the go
clipping this and tying that
tidying up the rows
finally he's done enough
he puts his tools back in the shed
thinks it's time to have a meal
have his daily bread
At end of day he takes a seat
to survey his domain
finally at peace within himself
panic gone again.

Butterfly Morning

In the morning
when all is still
and sleep is in your eyes
I gaze at your face
and think of butterflies

You slowly wake
you smile at me
inside my heart cries
you tell me you love me
and I think of butterflies

I hold you close
safe in my arms
you give a contented sigh
sun shines through the window
and I think of butterflies

You kiss my lips
so soft and sweet
tell me love will never die
you give me one last smile
and I think of butterflies

Mixed up Murder

It was murder, no doubt about it
you could tell by the look on his face
he was lying in a pool of blood
of the killer there was no trace

He was known to keep bad company
liked to gamble smoke and drink
he was always annoying his neighbours
didn't care what they might think.

To him she was just a one night stand
like plenty of others before
the list of his women was endless
his house had a revolving door.

They thought that a woman had killed him
her perfume still scented the air
her weapon was small and deadly
her stockings she'd left on a chair.

But the killer wasn't a woman
it was really a man in drag
who thought he'd met a like minded friend
until he'd called him a "fag."

The victim had only himself to blame
he'd been beguiled by a pair of blue eyes
a tight low cut dress and killer high heels
he didn't see through her disguise.

Some words can really wound you
make you lash out in hurt and pain
she'd stabbed him once through the heart
then walked home in the pouring rain.

Only One Shoe

A body was drifting down the river
a woman that somebody knew
she'd been floating about for hours
She was wearing only one shoe

A man who was crossing the bridge
looked down and watched her pass by
he stared at her in confusion
just couldn't believe his eyes

How did she get there he wondered
had suicide been on her mind
or had someone done this to her
left her for others to find?

Her hair spread out behind her
like a halo around her head
the man on the bridge felt so sad
oh how had she ended up dead?

He should have called for help
but what could anyone do?
He picked up a taxi to take him home
on the floor lay a single shoe

Tea the Panacea

Not tea, that panacea
for all that ails
nor my quietly whispered prayer
is taking away these feelings
as I sit in this chair and stare

I stare at the walls that were
once filled with paintings
but now lie stacked on the floor
I sit and look at the view from the window
and know I should walk out the door

The house is empty you are long gone
I try in vain to recall
all the love we once shared
but can only remember
when I realised you didn't care

I put on my coat my scarf and gloves
take a sip of the tea that's now cold
I say goodbye to the chair
and walk out the door
to breathe in the cold night air

The Bees Farewell

Down in the garden under the trees
the insects are gathered to welcome the bees
The nectar so thick clings to their legs
to make lots of honey to fill up the kegs.

Tonight in the garden they'll be such a ball
the insects will gather come one come all
They'll dance and drink the honey so sweet
and smile at each other and bow when they meet

Butterflies dance as the grasshopper plays
music so lively it blows you away
Ladybirds whirling around and around
beating their wings in time to the sound

The summer is ending the harvest is here
the insects are happy and full of good cheer
They've drank all the honey it's time for goodbyes
as the bees say farewell and return to their hives

Autonomy

These thoughts are mine and mine alone
no one can change my mind
henceforth I will my own way go
I've loosed the ties that bind

I care not for your hopes and dreams
not a jot you cared for mine
now I've excised you from my life
within my heart doth shine

It concerns me not your feelings hurt
I remember how that felt
I trained myself to not be weak
bade my soft heart not to melt

You wanted all decisions yours
mine you tossed aside
now you've gone I rule supreme
no more you will deride

To the winner goes the spoils
within I am content
I've held fast to my deep beliefs
my life will be well spent.

Had Enough?

When you've had enough of everyone
their troubles and their moans
when the last thing that you want to hear
is the ringing of your phone
Yes it's nice to help out others
when they're crying in despair
but sometimes you could strangle them
feel like pulling out your hair

Just tell yourself that you need time
for a little relaxation
let the others go to hell
they're just an irritation
Don't let the buggers grind you down
with their worries and their woes
if they keep annoying you
then tell them where to go

There's a lovely little phrase
that I use to great effect
and to ensure they get the message
I use the local dialect
I take a stance, stand straight and tall
give a little cough
and with two fingers held aloft
I tell them to just "Fuck Off."

The Perfume of Angels.

The perfume of Angels is heady and sweet
scenting the air all around
enticing the spirit to realms ever higher
with vibrations of heavenly sound

Aromas alluring pervade all the senses
evocative of earthly delights
they linger as long as the Angels are near
With halo's all shiny and bright

A rainbow arises to brighten the sky
its hue's softly merging together
and cherubs on clouds floating around
use the suns golden rays as a tether

Fragrances fill all the earth's holy places
lead us to a world filled with love
Wafting along in the breeze left behind
by the Angels who entice us above.

Fishing for Compliments

My man he is a fisherman
keen as keen can be
no matter what the weather's like
I know where he will be
He's got rods and nets and bait
and he's even got a boat
he'll sit and fish for hours on end
wearing his old green coat
He sits upon the riverbank
as patient as can be
I only wish he was half as patient
when he's dealing with me
I'm not a moaning wife
I've got interests of my own
when he's safely on the riverbank
you'll find me on the phone -
Arranging to meet my man friend
at his lovely little chalet
we've been meeting for a while now
and we've gotten very pally
He wants me to leave my man
and go and stay with him
but I haven't made my mind up yet
even though he's fit and trim
I think I'll hedge my bets a while
and take things nice and slow
and when I get tired of eating fish
I'll know it's time to go.

Beg me

I want your body close again
we've been apart far too long
come back to my waiting arms
that's where you belong
Just admit that you want me
what we have is rare
I'll give you all you need
but I definitely won't share
remember how it used to be
when we were both together
we always made the sparks fly
God I love you in leather
I want to run my hands all over you
strip you till you're bare
I want to make you beg for more
run my fingers through your hair
I'll lick that spot beneath your ear
kiss you till you scream
when you're back inside me
I'll be the cat that's got the cream

Tattoo

A tattoo was what she wanted
something tasteful and discreet
a flower upon her shoulder
or angel wings on her feet

She felt a bit embarrassed
but the tattooist was understanding
said even though she was seventy two
she wasn't too old for branding

She decided on a flower
a pansy to be precise
a little purple one she thought
might look rather nice

It was a little painful
but she soon got over that
she loved her little pansy
often gave it a little pat

A couple of weeks later
she went back to get another
this time it was a little heart
and inside it said "Mother"

Soon she got another one
a lovely butterfly
then it was a dragon
climbing up her thigh

Her life was full of colour now
she wanted more and more
but she knew she had to draw a line
she now had twenty-four

She decided on just one more
a message it could send
the tattooist thought it hilarious
when he tattooed
"The End"

Printed in Great Britain
by Amazon